TALKING ABOUT

Fostering and Adoption

Sarah Levete

Franklin Watts
London • Sydney

© Aladdin Books Ltd 2005

Designed and produced by
Aladdin Books Ltd
2/3 Fitzroy Mews
London W1T 6DF

First published in
Great Britain in 2005 by
Franklin Watts
96 Leonard Street
London EC2A 4XD

ISBN: 0 7496 6256 5

Design: PBD; Flick, Book
Design and Graphics

Picture research:
Pete Bennett & Rebecca Pash

Editor:
Rebecca Pash

The consultant, Shaila
Shah, is Director of
Publications for the British
Association of Adoption &
Fostering (BAAF).

Contents

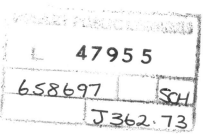

"What's my family like?"

There are many different types of family. Do you live with your birth parents, the mum and dad you were born to? Perhaps your family is just you and one of your birth parents. You might be part of a step family.

Sometimes, birth or step-parents are unable to care properly for their children. When this happens, the children may stay with another family, looked after by foster carers or adoptive parents.

Whichever family you belong to, the most important thing is to feel loved, safe and happy.

In a foster family, foster carers look after and love a child until he or she can safely return home to Mum and Dad. If you are adopted, you live with adoptive parents who look after and love you for always, just as if you had been born to them.

You might be fostered or adopted or you may know someone who is. This book talks about fostering and adoption. It explains what happens and helps you understand how everyone involved may feel.

"Why is someone fostered?"

There are many reasons why a child is fostered. It may be that their mum or dad has problems with alcohol or drugs, or suffers from emotional difficulties. The birth or step-parents may have hurt or mistreated their child.

A child is sometimes fostered if his or her mum or dad becomes very unwell. Some children with very special physical or emotional needs may be fostered for a while.

If a mum or dad cannot fully care for his or her child, the child may need to be fostered for a while.

If birth parents are unable to look after their child properly, a person called a social worker arranges for the child to stay with foster carers. The social worker makes regular visits throughout the child's stay to make sure things are OK. He or she will discuss when and if the child can return home.

Did you know...

Being fostered is sometimes called being "in care" or "looked after". Some foster children live with foster carers for a long time. Others stay for just a few weeks. Disabled children sometimes stay with a foster family to give their birth parents a short break. Whenever possible, foster children return to live with their birth parents.

"What will my foster family be like?"

A foster family may be made up of just one foster carer or a couple. They may have children of their own who become your foster brothers and sisters. If possible, you will be fostered with your birth brothers or sisters. Your social worker can also arrange for you to see other members of your family. Over time, you may stay with several different foster families.

Foster carers are there to make you feel safe and secure when there are problems at home.

Think about it

It's not easy being fostered – and it's not easy having parents who foster! If your parents foster, you may resent sharing your home and your parents' attention.

Chat to your parents about your feelings. Remember, there are loads of plus points! You'll make some great friends and it feels good to help others through difficult times.

Only people who can provide a safe and caring home are allowed to become foster carers. Social workers make sure that foster carers are able to offer the love and support you may need during your stay. You only meet your foster family when you go to live with them so there's a lot to get used to. It can take some time to settle in. But during your stay, your foster carers will treat you like the rest of the family, and help you feel at home.

"How does it feel to be fostered?"

Many children who are fostered will have experienced great upset. You may have been hurt or have a parent who is unwell. Staying with a new family may feel strange and overwhelming at first. Try to be patient, it can take a while to get used to different rules, routines and ways of doing things. Talk to your foster carers if you feel unsure.

It can take time to get used to living with a new foster family.

You may feel confused and sad about the problems that led to your fostering. You may feel angry and miss your mum or dad. These feelings are quite natural. Remember that foster carers only look after you until your birth parents can properly care for you again. Enjoying your time with foster carers doesn't stop you loving your mum and dad.

My story

"My sister and I lived with a foster family for a while when Mum couldn't manage. Our foster mum and dad were great and treated us just like their own children. We could always tell our social worker about any problems and she still checks up on us. We're back with our mum now, who's finding it much easier to cope."
Thomas

"Why is someone adopted?"

There are many reasons why a child is adopted. It can happen to children of any age, from all nationalities and cultures. If one or both birth parents dies, a child may be adopted. Step-parents might adopt their step-children so they have the same rights as birth parents. A baby may be adopted at birth if the parents are unable to care for him or her. If a child in foster care cannot return home, he or she is sometimes adopted.

Adoptive parents will look after and love their child as their own.

Think about it

The birth parents of an adopted child have no rights over the child's life. Sometimes, children can have contact, perhaps by post or phone, with their birth parents and other relatives. For others, it's best not to have any contact. Each situation is different and grown-ups such as social workers discuss what is best with each child.

Whatever the reason for adoption, adoptive parents care for and love their child as if they had been born to them. Adoption is not temporary – as long as the child is happy, they become part of the new family, forever.

"Who can adopt?"

Some people adopt because they cannot have children of their own, or because they would like a larger family. Adopting a child is a huge step, and not just anyone can do it. People who adopt have to show social workers and adoption agencies that they can offer a child a safe and loving home. Children waiting to be adopted have often been treated badly, and may need lots of extra care and attention. Adoptive parents need to have plenty of love and kindness to share.

A relative can adopt a child, as long as he or she is the best person for the job.

Just like any other family, adoptive families come in all shapes and sizes. There may be one or two adoptive parents, or even two dads or two mums. A step-parent or a relative such as a grandma can adopt a child.

Whoever adopts, the most important thing is that they offer love, safety and well-being.

Think about it

"My parents are adopting a ten-year-old boy called Hashim. He's had a really tough time at home and stayed with several different foster families – but now he's coming to live with us! I'm really excited about having a brother and I'm going to make sure Hashim feels like part of the family."   Sunita

"What happens?"

An adoption agency and a social worker make sure that the most suitable home is found for each child. They will consider the needs of both the adoptive parents and the child waiting to be adopted.

It can take a long time to find the right family to adopt a child. But when the right family and child are matched, a court hands over responsibility for the child to the adoptive parents.

A social worker makes sure a child is happy with his or her new family.

My story

"At last I've got a new family! Yesterday I went to meet them for the first time. I was really nervous but excited too. They live quite near where I go to school, so I won't have to change schools. I'm going to move in with them forever in a few weeks. I'm going to have a big sister as well as a new mum and dad!"   Elsa

While waiting for adoption, a child may stay with foster carers. Once they are adopted, he or she may need to move to a new area, and possibly a new school.

"How will I fit in with my new family?"

When you are adopted, you become a part of the new family. You probably take the family's surname. The family's uncles, aunts and grandparents become your uncles, aunts and grandparents. You may look different from your new family, but you belong to them, just as they belong to you.

Your adoptive family is chosen to make sure that you feel welcome and understood.

An adoptive family often shares a similar culture, religion and language as their adopted child. This makes it easier for you to feel at home. When this is not possible, parents are chosen who will understand and appreciate your language, and cultural and religious background. All adoptive parents are encouraged to help you understand and respect your own cultural identity.

Did you know...

Every year, about 300 children are adopted from overseas into the UK. These children have often suffered great poverty or lost their parents in war. Leaving their country in terrible circumstances can be extremely traumatic and their adoptive family needs to be especially supportive and loving.

"How does it feel to be adopted?"

If you were adopted at a very young age, your adoptive family is all that you know and remember. At first you may not even know you are adopted – being told can be a big shock.

Many children feel hurt and rejected by their birth parents. These feelings are natural. Try to remember that your birth parents made the difficult decision to have you adopted, believing that others could offer you a better home.

You can have feelings for both your adoptive and birth families.

Even if you hardly remember your birth parents, it's OK to have feelings for them, whether it's anger, sorrow or love. It's easier to deal with these feelings if you can express them. Try writing them down, or talk to your adoptive parents or close friends.

Think about it

Your birth brothers and sisters may have been adopted into the same family as you. If they are with other families, your social worker can arrange for you to stay in touch. If birth brothers and sisters stayed with your parents when you were adopted you may feel resentful and rejected. Talk to your adoptive parents or other grown-ups about your feelings.

"Where do I belong?"

It can be especially difficult to be adopted at an older age. As well as getting used to leaving one family, you have to adjust to a new family with new ways of doing things, and maybe even a new school. You may miss your birth family or your foster family and feel let down that you cannot stay with them. You may also be coming to terms with the difficult circumstances that led to your adoption.

It's natural to feel unsure and confused when you are adopted. In time, these feelings pass.

You may feel that you will never properly be part of your adoptive family and that you will be second best. But this is not true. Remember that, just as you joined your new family, they also joined you. You were adopted because your new family wanted to give you love, and to have your love.

Think about it

Whatever your feelings, sharing them will help. Talk to your parents, or a teacher. Keep a special notebook in which to write down your thoughts. It's OK to miss and love your birth parents. Being with your adoptive family doesn't mean you have to forget your past. It helps to think of your adoption as a new chapter in your life.

"What about my birth family?"

If you have no memory or knowledge of your birth family, you may start to feel curious about them. Your adoptive parents will tell you what they know. Later in life you may decide to find out more about your birth family. Talk to your adoptive parents about this – they may feel anxious that you will no longer consider them to be your parents.

Your adoptive parents will tell you as much as they know about your birth parents.

Think about it

People need to think carefully before trying to trace or contact their birth family. It's a huge decision. There are questions to consider such as: how will you feel if your birth parent doesn't want to see or talk to you? What if he or she is not what you expected? What do you hope for from finding your birth parents? Sometimes, teenagers or adults meet their birth parent/s and develop good relationships. But it is not always straightforward.

Finding out more about your birth parents cannot take away the care and love that your adoptive parents have given you.

"Why is it difficult for me sometimes?"

There may be times when you will feel very aware of being fostered or adopted. For instance, birthdays might remind you of your birth parents. Sometimes, others may make unkind comments about being fostered or adopted. However hurtful, try to ignore such remarks – they are made by people who don't know what they are talking about!

Family arguments are just part of growing up and usually have nothing to do with being fostered or adopted.

It's easy to blame any problems at home on being fostered or adopted, but remember that all families have ups and downs.

Your foster carers or adoptive parents are getting used to you as well! Parenting may be new to them, so make an effort to get to know them and talk to them about how you feel.

Think about it

Many adopted children look very different from their adoptive parents. This can feel hard, especially if others make comments about how similar the parents and birth children look. But feeling loved and happy is more important than having the same shaped nose!

"How can I move on?"

You have two families, both of whom you can love. Your birth parents gave you life and your foster or adoptive parents show you love. You can have good memories of your birth family and your past. And you can have a new life with your adoptive family. Why not celebrate your adoption day, just as you celebrate your birthday? It can help you and your new family feel special and have a sense of belonging.

Try making a life story using words, pictures and photos that chart your life from your birth to the present day. If you have no knowledge or photos of your birth family, simply write down or draw your thoughts and feelings.

If you are fostered or adopted, your start in life may not have been easy. But finding a loving foster or adoptive family is a time to love and be loved.

Did you know...

What have the following people got in common?

A Superman
B Charlotte Church
C Bill Clinton
D Ice T
E Eddie Murphy
F Seal
G Oprah Winfrey

A, B & C were adopted; D, E, F & G were all fostered.

"What can I do?"

• If you are fostered or adopted, remember that there are many types of family. Yours is no less a family than any other type.

• Talk to people about your feelings – they will understand what you are going through.

• If you know someone who is fostered or is waiting for adoption, think about how he or she may feel. They may be going through difficult times.

• If you know someone moving foster homes, or waiting for adoption, make a special effort to include him or her in games.

Be supportive of those who are going through difficult times.

Books on fostering & adoption

If you want to read more, try:

Adoption, What It Is and What It Means
by Shaila Shah, BAAF
Fostering, What It Is and What It Means
by Shaila Shah, BAAF
*My Parents Picked Me! A first look at
adoption* by Pat Thomas and Lesley Harker
Adoption is for Always
by Linda Warlvoord Grard

Contact information

If you want to talk to someone who doesn't
know you, these organisations can help:

British Association for Adoption
and Fostering (BAAF)
Skyline House, 200 Union Street,
London SE1 0LX
Tel: 020 7593 2000
The UK's leading charity working for
children separated from their birth families.

Childline
Tel: 0800 1111
A 24-hr free helpline for children.

On the Web

These websites are also helpful:

www.childline.org.uk

www.baaf.org.uk

www.rhrn.thewhocarestrust.org.uk/wct/
user/oi/index.jsp

www.rhrn.thewhocarestrust.org.uk/
carezone.htm

www.careleaversreunited.com

www.jigsaw.org.au

www.create.org.au/

**There is lots
of information
about fostering
and adoption
on the internet.**

The Who Cares? Trust
Kemp House, 152-160 City
Road, London, EC1V 2NP
Helpline: 0500 564570
Works to improve public care for
young people separated from their families.

Create Foundation, Australia
PO Box 313, Strawberry Hills, NSW 2012
Tel: 61 (0)2 9310 4234
Foundation of opportunities for children in care.